The Writing Template Book

The Writing Template Book

The MICHIGAN Guide to Writing Well and Success on High-Stakes Tests

Kevin B. King
Northern Essex Community College
New Hampshire Community Technical College

Foreword by Ann M. Johns
San Diego State University

Ann Arbor
THE UNIVERSITY OF MICHIGAN PRESS

ISBN-10: 0-472-03193-7
ISBN-13: 978-0-472-03193-1
Published in the United States of America
The University of Michigan Press
Manufactured in the United States of America

⊛ Printed on acid-free paper

2010   2009   2008   2007   4   3   2   1

FOREWORD

During my more than 30 years of teaching writing to international, bilingual, Generation 1.5, and other students, I have been introduced to, and attempted, all of the major pedagogical approaches. In the 1950s and early '60s, when the teaching of writing became an issue separate from the teaching of language, we were introduced to the current-traditional methods, product-based approaches in which focus on correct form dominated our work (see Johns 1997). When writing mattered and wasn't just a reflection of speech (see the audiolingual method), we were interested, first of all, in perfect representations of words and sentences. Weiderman (2000) refers to this period in language teaching history as "scientific": teachers "proceeded in a lockstep fashion, teaching bits of language from the grammatically simple to the grammatically more complex" (5). Our colleagues in first language composition and the work in contrastive rhetoric also introduced us to simple discourse forms. Comparison-contrast, cause-effect, and narrative were three forms that we taught, in a lockstep manner, as structures for essays. There seemed to be only one ESL (and novice student) composition book, *American English Rhetoric* by Robert Bander, published by Holt, Rinehart, and Winston, that we were given to use in our composition classes. A typical chapter title was "The Expository Composition: Developed by Comparison and Contrast."

Influenced in the 1960s by world events and remarkable changes in the United States, we began to question the approaches that concentrated solely on form and correctness, considering them to be too constraining for the students we were attempting to liberate. Thus, there occurred in composition instruction (and elsewhere) a major paradigm shift: from focus on perfect sentences and perfectly structured texts to the students, writers drafting and redrafting their assignments to solve rhetorical problems through texts. The learner-centered "process" movement, which continues to be basic to many composition programs, concentrated its efforts upon developing the learners' search for meaning and their writing processes. Rather than devoting time to perfection in student writing and stamping out errors, the teachers encouraged meaning-making, drafting, revising, and redrafting, all taking place in a collaborative environment where students peer reviewed each other's work. Students were encouraged throughout the process to reflect, thus developing a metacognitive awareness of their individual ways of approaching, and solving, their rhetorical problems. For some students and many teachers the process movement has, in fact, been liberating. As we now know so well, perfection and form are not all there is to successful writing.

However, there's another side of the process story that needs to be considered as we teach novice and second language students, many of whom do not yet control the registers or syntax of academic or professional Englishes. Jim Martin (1985), an Australian theorist, argues that the process movement has benefited only certain groups of students: those who are sufficiently familiar with the text products ("the genres") required in professional or academic context. Martin maintains that process approaches "promote a situation in which only the brightest, middle-class, monolingual students will benefit" (61) since they are the ones who have already begun to be initiated by their families or their elite schools into the academic and professional discourse communities they plan to enter. As Anyon (1980) and others have noted, most schools are already structured by social class, preparing selected students for certain types of professional lives. Support of these class disparities has no place in our composition programs.

So what do we do? We attempt, in some way, to close the gaps among rich, middle class, and poor as well as between those who speak and write English in various registers with ease and those who don't. In the theory and practice that is typical of post-process methodologies, a variety of pedagogies designed to achieve these ends have been developed. Some of those efforts follow the work of the New Rhetoricians in North America (see, e.g., Coe 2002), individuals who believe that to understand writing, a person must first understand the context and community in which the writing takes place. Others, such as the Australians and English for Specific Purposes practitioners, argue that we must teach the functional relationships between what a text should do linguistically and its purposes for the communities in which it will be read or published. In the Australian context (see Feez 1998), curricula have been designed to demonstrate these functional relationships at the text ("genre") and sentence levels. Both text structure and syntax are shown as contributing to success of a text in a specific context.

The Writing Template Book addresses the needs of students who are preparing for high-stakes assessments in contexts where they have little time to consider their writing processes. It provides for students and teachers three types of templates: the *thesis*, the *introduction/ roadmap*, and the *summary*, representing three essential elements in essay structures that are frequently required in high-stakes examinations, nationally (the SAT®), internationally (the TOEFL® iBT), and more locally, in many city, state, and provincial examinations. Initially, this volume will be useful for novice and ESL/EFL students as they attempt to write under these timed, and stressful, assessment situations. However, the volume can also provide the "training wheels" for writing sentences and paragraphs in a variety of genres for a variety of contexts. Throughout, the author makes the connections between essential discourse functions of essays and other genres (e.g., introduction, argument) and the structures of sentences and paragraphs that work. He provides a number of syntactic possibilities (see, e.g., Conclusion Templates) that teachers (and students) can vary according to prompts or tasks. He demonstrates how these templates can assist students to produce a text that is comprehensible even if errors are made (Roadmap Template Examples with Student Errors, pages 49–51). Fully as important are the vocabulary alternatives, some of which are quite sophisticated. In the *Do you Think* Introduction Template (page 45), for example, the author lists seven adjectives (*fascinating, difficult, tough, thought-provoking, interesting, multi-dimensional,* and *provocative*), each of which has a somewhat different semantic value. This type of exercise enables teachers and students to examine the differences among the choices, thereby indicating author stance on the issue (see Hyland 2005).

As Kevin B. King notes in his introduction, "one size does not fit all." This book cannot possibly illustrate the large variety of sentences that fulfill the functions in written texts. However, what it will do for students—and do it well—is get them started, giving them opportunities to explore the syntax, vocabulary, and functions of sentences and paragraphs in the assessments that determine their futures.

Using this volume, teachers can

- introduce and encourage student practice of one or more possibilities in an essential functional category (e.g., Proposition Template, Hedged Disagreement), varying the language and syntax as the students become more proficient
- select one of the sentences produced by students in their practice and work through a paragraph that follows from that sentence

- assist students in modifying the sentences produced to respond to new, but related, prompts
- encourage students to find examples of sentences and paragraphs that serve the same function in authentic texts from the worlds in which they live
- help students to continue to practice sentence variation, particularly in response to a variety of tasks and prompts—so that eventually they will not need the training wheels provided in this volume

As I attend conferences such as that on College Composition and Communication (CCCC) and talk to my colleagues who teach native speakers, I notice that textbooks with templates that serve rhetorical functions have entered their worlds, as well. *The Writing Template Book* is an excellent contribution to our pedagogical worlds, particularly for our novice and ESL students who are preparing for high-stakes examinations.

Ann M. Johns, San Diego State University
September 2006

References

Anyon, Jean. "Social Class and the Hidden Curriculum of Work." *Journal of Education* 162, no. 1 (Fall 1980).

Coe, Richard M. "The New Rhetoric of Genre: Writing Political Briefs." In *Genre in the Classroom: Multiple Perspectives*, ed. Ann M. Johns. Mahwah, NJ: Lawrence Erlbaum, 2002.

Feez, Susan. *Text-Based Syllabus Design*. Macquarie University: National Centre for English Language Teaching, 1998.

Hyland, Ken. "Stance and Engagement: A Model of Interaction in Academic Discourse." *Discourse Studies* 7 (2005): 173–92.

Johns, Ann M. *Text, Role, and Context: Developing Academic Literacies*. New York: Cambridge University Press, 1997.

Martin, Jim. *Factual Writing: Exploring and Challenging Social Reality*. New York: Oxford University Press, 1985.

Weiderman, A. "L2 Writing: Subpresses, a Model for Formulating Empirical Findings." *Learning and Instruction* 10 (2000): 73–99.

CONTENTS

CONCLUSION TEMPLATES 69

BODY OF PAPER TEMPLATES 91

SUMMARY TEMPLATE 96

INTRODUCTION FOR STUDENTS

➔ WHAT ARE WRITING TEMPLATES?

Most simply stated, templates are models. More specifically, writing templates are skeletal syntactic frameworks—parts of sentences or paragraphs with blanks to fill in with words of your choice. They are valuable because they help the reader understand better what you are saying. They help you, the writer, with organization, and they help you to develop the kinds of sentence, paragraph, and paper structure that strong writers display. They are also a guaranteed tool for getting better scores or grades on standardized writing tests or on class papers. Why do I say "guaranteed"? Because the syntax (the way words are put together in phrases and sentences) is error-free and the diction is at a high level, so the inclusion of the template will improve the way that your writing is received, the impression that will be left with your reader.

➔ WHY DO YOU NEED TEMPLATES?

Templates are needed because most writing teachers and textbooks simply give you advice on how to write. They don't show you exactly *how to do it*. Let's say you are someone who has never played golf and has never seen golf played. You could read a book about how to hit a golf ball, but when you actually tried to do it, you would have a very difficult time. Now what if a teacher not only let you see someone hit a golf ball, but also put his or her arms around yours and guided you through the correct motions? This is exactly the kind of hands-on support that templates can provide.

When you have read and written thousands of papers, you develop these templates. But this process takes a very long time. Using writing templates is a shortcut to that proficiency, a shortcut helpful if you are a non-native speaker of English or if you have not already mastered writing. After using templates a number of times, the syntax will implant itself automatically in your head, and eventually it will become second nature to use these syntactic frameworks.

➡ WHAT ABOUT STANDARDIZED TESTS LIKE THE SAT® AND THE TOEFL®?

Templates impose a structure, so your writing is better organized. In addition, the grammar and vocabulary in the templates automatically elevate the level of your writing. As a result, most student writers benefit from going into the SAT® or TOEFL® armed with a few templates.

While we know that graders and raters of these tests use specific criteria when evaluating, we also know that they read very quickly and develop a holistic impression of a piece of writing—an impression that is significant when assigning a score. We also know that vocabulary and diction are a large part of what goes into the forming of that holistic impression, which is all the more reason to use templates. In fact, some graders report confidentially that they read only the introduction and conclusion, and they may be very impressed by the implicit organization of the introduction, as well as by the template conclusion. Many writing teachers might agree that they do the same thing when reading essays—that they don't need to read the whole paper to know student level or evaluate the writing. As a result, you should go into the SAT® having memorized a **thesis sentence template,** an **introduction/roadmap template,** and a **conclusion template.** For the TOEFL®, you should also have a **summary** template. The work you put into memorizing these will pay off. Don't panic if you can't remember the templates completely; using only part of a template will be of significant value. Before you start writing your essay or even read the question, write your templates either on a computer screen or on one of the pieces of scrap paper given to you. Then read the question and begin your writing.

An *LA Times* editorial writer and test-grader offers this advice: "Prepare a few highly burnished words that can be applied to almost any situation. A prepared sentence or two wouldn't hurt. One essay struck me with its well-wrought line: 'It may be the case, then, that secrecy has its own time and place in our vast world.' I was dazzled by the calm maturity of that sentence until I realized it could well have been composed in advance. No matter. I gave the kid credit for planning" (Klein, "How I Gamed the SAT®," 3 April 2005).

Before we close, a word of caution is in order. With templates, as with clothes, one size does not fit all. That is—you can't just plug your topic into the right place and expect the template to work perfectly. The template is not an intelligent computer. At times you need to change the syntax or the word form (e.g., make an adjective a noun). Usually, this is pretty obvious and easy to do. However, errors will be made. But even with an error in the syntax, your essay will be superior to what it would have been without using the template.

In conclusion, writing templates will help bridge the gap between you and the advanced writer. They can make you a more confident and better writer, which will serve you well in your work beyond tests and courses.

➥ How Do the Template Options Work?

When there are columns of options, any word in one column can go with any option in another column.

_____ **are the** _____ **breakfast food.**

Croissants	most delicious
Eggs	best
Donuts	healthiest

For instance, in this template there are nine different combinations that can be used. *Croissants* may be used not only with *most delicious.* You have three options with *croissants,* as you do with *donuts* and with *eggs*. You could write:

Croissants **are the** most delicious **breakfast food.**
> or

Croissants **are the** best **breakfast food.**
> or

Croissants **are the** healthiest **breakfast food.**

Similarly, you could write:

Eggs **are the** most delicious **breakfast food.**
> or

Eggs **are the** best **breakfast food.**
> or

Eggs **are the** healthiest **breakfast food.**

Or:

Donuts **are the** most delicious **breakfast food.**
> or

Donuts **are the** best **breakfast food.**
> or

Donuts **are the** healthiest **breakfast food.**

INTRODUCTION FOR TEACHERS

What a pleasant surprise to find that one is not alone. Prior to the national TESOL convention in 2005, I had thought that using writing templates was my own idiosyncratic response to my students' inability to use the instruction and correction they had been given to produce reasonable papers. By *template* I mean a skeletal syntactic framework that can be used to craft a roadmap/introduction, a conclusion, a summary, or the body of an analytic paper. In giving that TESOL presentation, I discovered that many teachers use and teach rudimentary templates. The after-session conversation became a kind of support group, among a dozen or so of us "closet-templatists" who had finally found one another. I left with an e-mail list two pages long of teachers hungry for more information on templates. Quite simply, they had seen that, despite all the instructions they gave students on how to write a conclusion or an introduction, the results almost never approached what they were after and what students needed to produce in their academic work. Many teachers turned to inventing their own templates, although they seldom called them that. I am happy to report that writing templates are now out of the closet, perhaps for good.

➔ GENERAL REMARKS

Few are born with the swing of Tiger Woods or Charlie Sifford, the first African American to "make it big" on the PGA tour. Sifford relates that as a teenager he picked up some clubs and within a week was shooting in the 70s. Sifford's golfing ability is clearly expressing one of Howard Gardner's multiple intelligences, and the ability to write could be another. While these abilities in some practitioners appear to be innate, the analogy of writing to golf is appropriate when we focus on the nature of the writing as science. One salient feature of the scientific process is replicability, a feature that figures significantly in templates. *One key to good golf is a reliable, replicable swing; one key to good writing is reliable, replicable syntax.*

On the Internet, one can obtain templates for letters of recommendation, refunds, reprimands, resignations, invitations, and a host of other rhetorical occasions. What does the marketplace tell us about the direction of our writing instruction in high school and college? One response is that templates are available for the kind of writing most people do in the real world—that is, past high school or college. At one time, one might have argued that these functions (recommendations, etc.) were part of what we should be training our students to perform. But in the Internet age, that argument is no longer robust. Students can easily find unimaginative, simplistic templates for these functions themselves. Another response might be that our writing instruction should be directed toward areas that templates do not address, primarily areas that involve thought, analysis, and argumentation. It is precisely these areas that I want to address, with templates in mind, to explore how our methods of writing instruction might profit from cross-fertilization via templates.

We already teach vocabulary, transitions, outlines, and even structure by means of a five-paragraph essay (whether you agree that the five-paragraph structure is valuable is irrelevant here). That structure is, arguably, a kind of template. What we have largely ignored or under-emphasized is help with the syntax necessary to create those larger structures. In effect, we say, "Here are the bricks *(vocabulary)*, the mortar *(transitions)*, and the scaffolding *(essay structure)*, now you put it together." Every architect learns reticulation (setting square stones on edge diagonally) from a master, a mentor, but writing students are left to their own devices to discover what the verbal equivalent of reticulation is. What I suggest is that we show students what this syntax consists of via templates that are general enough to be used in virtually any structured essay, which differentiates them from the templates for specific functions (recommendations, etc.) that have been mentioned.

While writing templates are of great value to students on standardized tests, they also have instructional benefits within the standard writing curriculum. First, they teach organization in a hands-on way. When students actually experience an imposed structure and practice using it, it tends to rub off. Further, noun clauses, inverted subject/verb order, subjunctives, and other difficult structures are scaffolded so that students can use them correctly. Idiomatic expressions that good writers use and that few non-native speakers of English and emerging native writers would ever use become a standard part of their writing repertoire.

My own complete conversion to templates occurred when I found myself lecturing for the nth time about stressing the limitations of one's work in a conclusion. Whereas the texts I had been using primarily taught that conclusions restate the main points, I had asked students to see their work as part of an intellectual continuum, where they were writing in the present, cited the past, and then in conclusion pointed to directions that further work could go, since they had not said all that could be said about any particular topic.

David Posner, writing in *Profession* (2005), concurs with this approach: "If we are able to conclude that while we may have learned something there is still more to be learned, we may mitigate some of the evil inherent in the idea of a conclusion and along the way do some good for both our readers and ourselves."[1]

While the majority of my students bought into the concept of stressing limitations in a conclusion, I very seldom saw the principle applied in their papers. It is clear to me that, if one wants results, it makes no more sense simply to talk about a concept, even with an example, than it does for Tiger Woods to tell a neophyte golfer how to swing, even with a demonstration. The neophyte golfer needs to get to the practice range with a club in hand and with the golf template:

> **Position your feet with respect to the ball here.**
>
> **Keep your left arm stiff here.**
>
> **Throw your hips into the ball here.**

Similarly, when I provided a template for the conclusion I had been advocating, almost all of my students used versions of it, and their conclusions were orders of magnitude better. An additional benefit of conclusion templates is that they teach something about tone as well as structure. The tone of these conclusion templates is humility, as opposed to the self-congratulation teachers more normally see.

➡ ART, CRAFT, OR SCIENCE?

Writing is often referred to as an art or as a craft. I want to stress the scientific aspect of writing, which means, simply, *syntax*. Putting words together is like putting bricks atop others. They go in patterns. The process is mostly mechanical and rarely artistic.

---

[1]David Posner, "Rhetonic, Redemption, and Fraud: What We Do When We End Books," *Profession*, no. 1 (2005), 180.

This claim does not come without some version of an Augustinian confession. I have felt at times like a philistine, an apostate, abandoning the "intern model" of teaching writing. What I mean by that is the typical long-term process of writing as an internship in the physician-apprentice sense—long hours and little sleep, along with the sense that, although the process was seriously flawed, unnecessarily harsh, and burdensome, the interns did it, emerging scathed but knowledgeable. Why shouldn't the new crop of interns be similarly brutalized?

In my view, it is unfortunately rare that the effort is made by students to dissect the syntactic structure of an argumentative or analytical essay. It is as if we expect students to intuit this structure magically or, in the humanities version of medical residency, expect our writer-interns to go through the same lengthy apprenticeship we did and to emerge as equally capable writers. But on the whole, this is a fantasy and does a gross disservice to the majority of student-writers who show the same disinclination toward writing that many of us with strong verbal intelligence have often felt toward math. We feel free to rail at how poorly math is taught but are similarly uncritical of the tedious and antiquated methodology often employed in teaching writing, the results of which are unsatisfactory to a growing number of writing teachers.

Caveat: Students need to note that one size does not fit all. They can't just plug a topic in the right place and expect the template to always work. Some syntax needs manipulation. Usually, this is easy. Will errors be made? Sure. But such syntax errors would probably be consistent with similar usage errors in the student's paper, and the resulting essay will still be superior to what would have been written without the template. Templates are no panacea. We still have to do our job. No matter what we teach students—citation, organization, or support for an argument—they will make mistakes from which they will learn. Templates are no different in this regard. And templates will be internalized; they will teach.

Some colleagues are worried that if template use becomes widespread, all papers will look alike. The cynic's response is that too many are already alike, in their incompetence. My answer is that while some, or even many, papers may bear syntactical resemblance in certain parts, for the most part, the papers will be better than what we are seeing now. Similarity wins, hands down, over incompetence. Good students will eventually develop their own templates. For them, however, the process of intuiting the syntax of an introduction/roadmap or a conclusion will be accelerated. We are training our students for the real world, where clarity and content are what count. No one ever complained that the scaffolding for all of Louis Kahn's buildings looked the same. The scaffolding comes off and you get the architecture; the syntax comes off in the readers' heads and they get the ideas.

Other colleagues have raised the question of plagiarism in templates. This is a non-starter. Plagiarism is most fundamentally the theft of ideas. There are no ideas here; there is only syntax, which in most cases is just parts of sentences. Templates are patterns, and no one owns a pattern that has been used millions of times. Even the rare short complete sentences in these templates have been used in their entirety tens, if not hundreds, of thousands of times. They are mainly transition sentences, acting like one-word transitions. Further, every template in this book came from another source. I didn't make them up. So no teacher can say, "That phrase, linked to that phrase, minus a few original words in between, further linked to that phrase came from Kevin King's book," for that author got the phrases from someone else. They are not mine, and they are not anybody else's. They belong to the English language. They are the linguistic commons, and everyone has a right to them. Moreover, numerous writing texts use rudimentary templates. *Ready to Write More*, a textbook by Karen Blanchard and Christine Root,[2] gives the following templates for topic sentences and thesis sentences:

	causes of
There are several	reasons for _____.
	effects of

One writing teacher at my former school advised using the following template in her written instructions for an essay: "A good model for the last sentences of your first paragraph would be:

This advertisement seems to be about _____ but is really about _____. I will argue that _____."

Obviously, these texts and teachers are not teaching anyone to plagiarize. The writing templates in this book are different from these examples only in that they are designed for specific parts of *any* essay students may write; they are much more comprehensive and more expansive, and they use more sophisticated language and structures.

---

[2]Karen Blanchard and Christine Root, *Ready to Write More: From Paragraph to Essay* (Upper Saddle River, NJ: Pearson, 2004).

⇒ TEMPLATES AND STANDARDIZED WRITING TESTS (SAT®, TOEFL®)

While the goal of writing templates is not simply to enhance scores on standardized tests, templates are very effective tools for such tests. I believe that students armed with templates will outperform a similar group of students without templates for a couple of reasons. First, organization is, while not assured, at least significantly enhanced by a roadmap template. At whatever point in the writing process students create a roadmap, referral to that segment will help the students to ascertain whether or not they have followed their plan. Second, graders of such tests, who are being paid a sum for each graded essay, generally allow themselves about three minutes to evaluate the writing. Some graders will look only at the introduction and the conclusion, the two areas where templates can be most useful. The writing there will be better and more impressive than in similar sections in the exams of students who do not have templates. While there is, as yet, no empirical evidence to support this claim, disbelievers would be hard-pressed to come up with more compelling reasons for the theoretical template-less group equaling or surpassing the performance of the template-armed group.

Caveat: Going into a standardized test situation, students may forget some or even much of the template they had hoped to use, but some skeleton of it will probably remain, so that a student may recall something like: *What I've argued here is . . .* and *Only furter studies will show . . . .* Just remembering a few components will result in students performing better than they would have without the template.

⇒ CONCLUDING REMARKS

I hope that writing teachers will expand the repertoire of their instruction by assigning essays for syntactical analysis, allowing students of all proficiency levels to discover on their own the syntactical structures of good essays. With that our story comes full circle, for those students will arrive at structures similar to the ones I have presented.

Only longitudinal study will prove or disprove what I think is the case—that students who use templates for various parts of their papers will eventually lose their need for templates, and that the various syntactic structures that comprise many good conclusions, introductions, etc., will be imprinted in the heads of the students who used templates to a much greater degree than in the heads of the students who never used them.

THESIS SENTENCE TEMPLATES

A **thesis sentence** is a sentence in the introduction that tells the reader what the topic or argument of the essay is. Experienced writers have little difficulty writing thesis sentences. This is because they have read and written thousands of them.

You, the *emerging writer*, don't have it so easy. So, you have to accelerate the process. You do this via **thesis sentence templates.** A thesis sentence template is the basic machinery of a thesis sentence, what makes it work. It is like a car minus the hood, the doors, the engine, the side panels, the wheels, and the air conditioner. On that basic structure, thousands of different cars can be built. From a thesis sentence template, thousands of thesis sentences can be constructed.

The introduction for any piece of writing is *very* important. This is where you establish a relationship with the reader. The introduction will always be read, while the body of the paper might sometimes be glossed over (not carefully read) by graders of standardized tests like the SAT® or TOEFL®.

➡ HOW THE THESIS SENTENCE TEMPLATES WORK

Each type of thesis sentence presented in this section is followed by two or three examples of how very different thesis sentences can be written using the template. Then you will write two or three thesis sentences of your own using the template. If you find the template difficult, just do one sentence on your own. But the more you practice, the better you will be at writing templates. Note that when suggestions for filling in the blanks are supplied, the small list represents just a fraction of the thousands of possible words you could use, as long it's the same part of speech.

By the time you finish writing your versions of all of the template sentences, the syntactic models that native speakers have in their heads will be more firmly implanted in your head. Any time you write an essay, review the templates. Keep a favorite in mind, one that you can use whenever you need it, especially when writing under the pressure of time constraints.

You are not expected to be able to use all of the thesis sentence templates successfully. The idea is for you to find a few that you can use and reuse with confidence. In preparation for a writing test, memorize a couple of them, and use the one that seems to fit the topic best.

If you cannot write your own variation of a template, that's **FINE!** It just means that that template is not for you. Forget about it. Concentrate on templates that you are comfortable with. Finding the right template is like finding the right pair of pants. You try them on until some fit.

→ I. COMPARISON/CONTRAST THESIS SENTENCES

These templates can be used for essays where you are instructed to compare and contrast.

Comparison/Contrast Template 1

> **The differences [similarities] between** _____
> **and** _____ **are** _____, **and they** _____
>
> pronounced   deserve
> striking   merit
>
> _____ _____.
>
> thorough   investigation
> rigorous   scrutiny
>   examination

Examples

The differences between college **and** high school **are** pronounced, **and they** deserve thorough investigation.

The similarities between R-rated movies **and** PG-rated movies **are** pronounced, **and they** merit rigorous scrutiny.

Your Thesis Sentences

1. _____

2. _____

3. _____

Comparison/Contrast Template 2

_____ **some** _____ **similarities,**

Although they bear   superficial
Despite bearing   minor

the differences between _____ **and** _____
are _____ **.**
     clear
     remarkable
     striking
     pronounced

Examples

Although they bear **some** superficial **similarities, the differences between** Athens **and** Sparta **are** clear.

Despite bearing **some** minor **similarities, the differences between** Pele **and** Ronaldinho **are** pronounced.

Your Thesis Sentences

1. _____

2. _____

3. _____

Comparison/Contrast Template 3

> **While some differences between** _____ **and** _____ **are**
> _____, **the similarities are** _____.
>
> evident   striking
> noticeable   pronounced
>   salient

Examples

While some differences between Japan **and** the United States **are** evident, **the similarities are** salient.

While some differences between high school **and** college **are** evident, **the similarities are** striking.

Your Thesis Sentences

1. _____

2. _____

3. _____

⇨ II. Proposition Thesis Sentences

The next eight templates are for use in responding to a **proposition**. A proposition is a statement that establishes the truth or falsity of something. This sentence not only clarifies your position—it establishes your mastery of some sophisticated syntax. These templates begin with noun clauses. A noun clause is a group of words that acts just like a noun, serving as a subject, an object of a verb, or an object of a preposition. Using a noun clause correctly will make a good impression on your reader.

Proposition: X is Y

Proposition Example: Democracy is the best form of government.
                             X   Y

Proposition Template 1 (Agreement)

This template can be used when you agree with the proposition.

The _____ that ___X___ is ___Y___ is a _____ one,

notion[1]	fascinating[2]
belief	an interesting
thought	thought-provoking
idea	provocative
proposition	

and one that I believe in.

Examples

The notion **that** democracy **is** the best form of government **is a** fascinating **one, and one that I believe in.**

The thought **that** world peace **will be**[3] attained in the next decade **is an** interesting **one, and one that I believe in.**

Your Thesis Sentences

1. (*proposition:* Secrecy* is bad.)

_____

_____

2. (*proposition:* America is a melting pot.**)

_____

_____

Secrecy means keeping secrets.

**Melting pot* is a common metaphorical description of the United States and its history, meaning that immigrants eventually melt into society so that one nationality can't be distinguished from another. This was especially popular in the early 1900s.

3. (Write your own sentence.)

_____

_____

Notes

1. *Of the alternatives in the first blank of the template, I prefer the word* notion. *It is a more abstract word than the others and sounds a bit more sophisticated.*
2. *There are* thousands *of adjectives that can be used in the last blank.*
3. *In the second example,* will be *is used instead of* is. *You can change tenses like this to fit your thesis.*

Proposition Template 2 (Disagreement)

This template can be used when you disagree with the proposition. Therefore, the adjective in the final blank has to be a negative one.

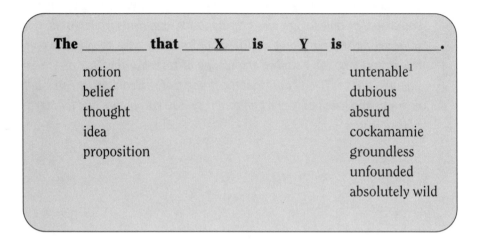

The _____ **that** ___**X**___ **is** ___**Y**___ **is** _____.

notion	untenable[1]
belief	dubious
thought	absurd
idea	cockamamie
proposition	groundless
	unfounded
	absolutely wild

Examples

The belief **that** the president can do anything he wants **is** groundless.

The idea **that** all men are created equal **is** dubious.

Your Thesis Sentences

1. (*proposition:* Hot dogs are the best food.)

   _____

   _____

2. (Write your own sentence.)

   _____

   _____

3. (Write your own sentence.)

   _____

   _____

Note

1. *The first two adjectives,* untenable *and* dubious, *represent mild disagreement. The others represent strong disagreement. In general, it is advisable to go with mild disagreement because questions are usually structured so that there are reasonable arguments on both sides, and if you strongly disagree, you should be able to pick apart the opposing arguments (you must do this to receive the best score), which should not be easy to do. However, researchers who have studied the scoring of tests like the Test of Written English® (TWE) or TOEFL® note that the strength of students' arguments is not nearly as important as their organization, syntax, vocabulary, and the length of their essays.*

Proposition Template 3 (Disagreement)

That ____**X**____ is ___**Y**___ is a/an _____ **proposition.**[1]

> dubious[2]
> suspicious
> problematic
> untenable
> egregious
> groundless
> unfounded
> absolutely wild

Examples

That democracy **is** the best form of government **is a** dubious **proposition**.

That the city of New Orleans can be restored to its condition prior to Hurricane Katrina **is an** untenable **proposition**.

Your Thesis Sentences

1. _____

_____

2. _____

_____

3. _____

_____

Notes

1. *This template begins with a noun clause. It is a sophisticated structure that will impress your reader.*
2. *Be sure to look up and understand each of these adjectives. The first three indicate mild disagreement, while the last five indicate strong disagreement.*

Proposition Template 4 (Disagreement)

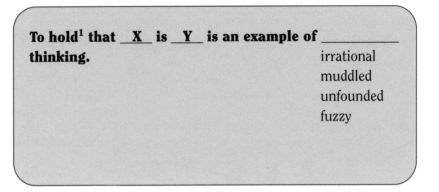

To hold[1] that __X__ is __Y__ is an example of _____
thinking.   irrational
                                              muddled
                                              unfounded
                                              fuzzy

Examples

To hold that learning a second language **is** easy **is an example of** fuzzy
thinking.

To hold that life **is** harder now than it was for our ancestors **is an**
example of muddled **thinking**.

Your Thesis Sentences

1. _____

   _____

2. _____

   _____

3. _____

   _____

Note

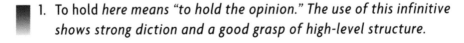

1. To hold *here means "to hold the opinion." The use of this infinitive*
   shows strong diction and a good grasp of high-level structure.

Proposition Template 5 (Disagreement)

> **To subscribe to the _____¹ that _____ is _____.**
>
> | belief | irrational |
> |---|---|
> | notion | indefensible |
> | proposition | absurd |
> | | nonsensical |

Examples

To subscribe to the belief **that** the world will come to an end tomorrow **is** absurd.

To subscribe to the notion **that** vitamin C can make you live to be one hundred **is** nonsensical.

To subscribe to the proposition **that** women are inferior to men **is** irrational.

Your Thesis Sentences

1. _____

_____

2. _____

_____

3. _____

_____

Note

1. To subscribe to X *means "to believe X."*

Proposition Template 6 (Hedged Disagreement)

This template is to be used when you want to qualify your stance—that is, when you want to disagree mildly. This is called **hedging.** It is often the wisest strategy in dealing with a proposition because your position is easier to defend.

> **That** _____ **is somewhat** _____.
>
> dubious
> suspicious
> problematic
> questionable

Examples

That diamonds are a girl's best friend **is somewhat** dubious.

That tax breaks for the rich will do great things for the economy **is somewhat** questionable.

That global warming is not occurring **is somewhat** problematic.

Your Thesis Sentences

1. _____

_____

2. _____

_____

3. _____

_____

Proposition Template 7

That _____ is a/an _____ proposition.

horrendous
attractive
appealing
fallacious

Examples

That cars can be made as cheaply in the United States as in China **is a** fallacious **proposition**.

That fuel made from corn can replace gasoline **is an** attractive **proposition**.

That robots will do all of our cleaning **is an** appealing **proposition**.

Your Thesis Sentences

1. _____

_____

2. _____

_____

3. _____

_____

Proposition Template 8

The _____ that _____ **seems to me to constitute**
    assertion
    denial

a fundamental _____ **about** _____.
      confusion
      misunderstanding
      mistake

Examples

The assertion **that** writing templates won't improve your test scores **seems to me to constitute a fundamental** mistake **about** their value.

The denial **that** international students need special help with their English **seems to me to constitute a fundamental** misunderstanding **about** the problems these students face.

The assertion **that** prescription drugs are fairly priced **seems to me to constitute a fundamental** confusion **about** the profit motive of pharmaceutical companies.

Your Thesis Sentences

1. _____

_____

2. _____

_____

3. _____

_____

➡ III. THESIS SENTENCES FROM PRIZE-WINNING ESSAYS

Thesis sentences taken or adapted from excellent high school essays follow. The sentences deal mainly with literature, specifically Shakespeare, but as you will see, the subject does not matter. Shakespeare is just one of the kinds of "cars" we talked about. These templates are presented in a rough order of difficulty; that is, the ones on pages 30–31 are harder than the ones on pages 25–29. <u>Remember</u>: If you find one or more templates too difficult, just omit them.

Thesis Sentence Template 1

It would be hard to claim that Milton was not a reader of Shakespeare.[1]

> **It would be hard to** _____ **that** _____.
>
> claim
> maintain
> prove
> show
> deny

Examples

It would be hard to prove **that** Einstein was not a genius.

It would be hard to maintain **that** civil war is good for a country.

It would be hard to deny **that** men make more money than women, even when doing the same job.

Your Thesis Sentences

1. _____

   _____

2. _____

   _____

3. _____

   _____

Note

1. *There is a simple rhetorical trick at work in this template, one that will impress your reader. The topic is in the that clause. The template takes a simple proposition, X is/was Y and transforms it into the more sophisticated structure, "It's hard to say that X is not/was not Y."*

Thesis Sentence Template 2

Hamlet's inaction, according to a common interpretation, is his tragedy.

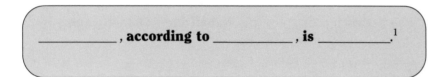

_____ , **according to** _____ , **is** _____.[1]

Examples

Hurricane Katrina's aftermath, **according to** the experts, **is** going to be devastating.

President Roosevelt's greatness, **according to** his admirers, **is** easy to see.

Alternative sources of energy, **according to** researchers, **will be**[2] increasingly important.

Your Thesis Sentences

1. _____

_____

2. _____

_____

3. _____

_____

Notes

1. *The rhetorical trick in this template is simply to take the most basic proposition, X is Y, and to add an interrupter,* according to_____. *The correct use of the interrupter impresses your audience.*
2. *In almost all templates, the verb tense can be changed to suit your purpose.* Is *can be changed to* will be *or* has been, *etc.*

Thesis Sentence Template 3 (Definition)

The definition of manhood is something not easily come by.[1]

> **The definition of _____ is something not easily come by.**[2]

Examples

The definition of sexuality **is something not easily come by.**

The definition of democracy **is something not easily come by.**

The definition of a liberal education **is something not easily come by.**

Your Thesis Sentences

1. _____

_____

2. _____

_____

3. _____

_____

Notes

1. Not easily come by *means "you don't find it easily." The diction impresses your reader because it is idiomatic and grammatically sophisticated.*
2. *Use this template any time you have to define something.*

Thesis Sentence Template 4

How are we to account for the recent crisis of obesity in America?[1]

> **How are we to account for** _____?[2]

Examples

How are we to account for the increase of carbon dioxide in our atmosphere?

How are we to account for the worldwide outbreaks of avian flu?

How are we to account for the rampant use of steroids in professional sports?

Your Thesis Sentences

1. _____

_____

2. _____

_____

3. _____

_____

Notes

1. *Asking a question is a good way to begin an essay or introduce your topic. This one can be used with almost any topic.*
2. How are we + *infinitive (Inf) is a sophisticated way of saying* How shall we + *verb (V).*

Thesis Sentence Template 5

The Merchant of Venice is a play about love and revenge; but it is also, more subtly, a play about parents and their children.

_____ **is** _____ **; but it is also, more** _____, _____.[1]

> importantly
> deeply
> significantly
> notably
> profoundly
> subtly
> obviously
> simply

Examples

Marriage **is** about love and commitment; **but it is also, more** simply, about getting along.

Being an immigrant **is** about leaving one's native country; **but it is also, more** deeply, about adapting to a new culture.

Drug addiction **is** a huge problem for the police; **but it is also, more** importantly, a significant problem for the addict and his or her family.

Your Thesis Sentences

1. _____ is _____; but it is also, more

_____, _____.

2. _____ is _____; but it is also, more

_____, _____.

3. _____ is _____; but it is also, more

_____, _____.

Note

1. *This template expresses a very simple idea:* X is Y, but it is also Z. *The correct use of the semicolon and the interrupter present this simple idea in a very impressive manner.*

Thesis Sentence Template 6 (Transformation)

In Graham Greene's The Power and the Glory, *the whiskey priest has undergone many important transformations, but none more so than his outlook on God's grace.*

_____ **has undergone** _____ _____ **transformations,**

a number of	important
numerous	significant
many	prominent

but none more so[1] than _____ .[2]

Examples

The United States **has undergone** numerous important **transformations, but none more so than** the ending of slavery.

Iraq has **undergone** many significant **transformations, but none more so than** the toppling of Saddam Hussein.

My job **has undergone** a number of prominent **transformations, but none more so than** the doubling of my work load while reducing my hours.

Your Thesis Sentences

1. _____ has undergone _____ transformations,

   but none more so than _____ .

2. _____ has undergone _____ transformations, but

   none more so than _____ .

3. _____ has undergone _____ transformations, but

   none more so than _____ .

Notes

1. So *refers to the previous adjective; that is* important, significant, prominent.
2. *Use this template for any topic that features a major change.*

INTRODUCTION TEMPLATES

Good introductions will have three components: *some general statement(s) and perhaps background about the topic, a thesis sentence, and a roadmap of where the paper is going.* The last of these, a roadmap, is optional, and in very short essays you do not need it. The term *roadmap* is metaphorical; it refers to the organization of your paper—what you will talk about and in what order. Unlike standard essay form in many countries (particularly in Europe), in the United States everything is stated at the beginning. There are no delicious surprises, no unexpected climaxes, and no suspense. Think of the prominent and often used American expression: *Show me the money!* Your American audience wants to see the most important things first. In effect, an introduction should be like a preview to a movie.

Although the introduction comes first in the essay, you do not have to write it first. You might start with your introduction template and then revise it after you finish because you seldom know everything you are going to say before you attempt to say it. Author and teacher Michael Schoenfeldt offers some similar and sage advice: "I confess that my most effective introductory gestures have come from elements recycled from failed conclusions—as if only after the manuscript is written do I have the authority and knowledge necessary to provide a proper introduction to my work."[1]

 ## I. GENERAL INTRODUCTION TEMPLATES

General Introduction Template 1

> **Truth be told,**[1] _____ has generated a lot of _____
>
>   interest
>   controversy
>   discussion
>
> _____.
> lately
> recently
> in recent years.
> in recent time

---

[1]Michael Schoenfeldt, "First Impressions and Last Thoughts," *Profession*, no. 1 (2005), 170–71.

> **The major** _____ **that I will address in this essay**
>
> topic(s)
> issue(s)
> point(s)
>
> **is/are:** _____ .

Question: Why have you selected Harrad College?

Example

Truth be told, Harrad College **has generated a lot of** interest lately. **The major** topics **that I will address in this essay are**[2]: the role of geography in my choice, the strength of the mathematics department, and the financial support offered by Harrad College.[3]

Notes

1. Truth be told _is an idiomatic expression meaning "if the truth is told." Since you are telling the truth, this is a good way to begin. The expression uses the subjunctive case, a rarity in English. Using the expression demonstrates a high level of diction and an understanding of advanced structure._
2. _In this case, you would use a colon (:) to introduce your list. If you have just one topic, then you do not have a list and therefore do not need a colon._
3. _Because your list represents the three paragraphs composing the body of your paper, your organization is clear and you do not need a roadmap template._

Question: Music is an important part of society. People like music for many different reasons. Why do you think music is such an important part of people's lives?

Example

> **Truth be told,** the part that music plays in people's lives **has generated a lot of** interest in recent times. **The major** topic **that I will address in this essay is**[1] why music is so important in people's lives.[2]

Notes

1. *You do not use a colon here because you do not have a list; you have one major topic. Of course, how you will address this topic will be part of your roadmap.*
2. *You have not mentioned any specifics of the body of your paper so you need a roadmap template now.*

Your Question: Your family just told you that it will send you to any country you want for the whole summer. What country would you like to visit for the whole summer? Why would you like to go there?

Your Example

_____

_____

_____

Your Question: Agree or disagree with the following statement: Smoking should be allowed in public places.

Your Example

_____

_____

_____

Simplified Introduction Template

> **Truth be told,** _____.
>
> **In the following paragraphs, I will**
>
> _____ **the** _____ **of** _____.
>
> | | |
> |---|---|
> | point out | role |
> | elucidate | importance |
> | illustrate | significance |
> | | consequences |

Question: Relate the most humorous experience in your life.

Example

Truth be told, I have had a lot of humorous experiences in my life. **In the following paragraphs, I will** point out **the** significance **of** an experience I had at the age of four.

Question: Parents are the best teachers for children. Do you agree or disagree with this statement?

Example

Truth be told, parents are not the best teachers for children. **In the following paragraphs, I will** elucidate **the** importance **of** grammar school teachers and high school teachers in the lives of children.[1]

Your Question: Some high schools require all students to wear the same uniforms. Do you think universities should also require students to wear the same uniforms?

Your Example

_____

_____

_____

Question: If you could change one important thing about your country, what would you change?

Your Example

_____

_____

_____

Note

1. *Again, a roadmap template is built into the introduction.*

General Introduction Template 2

The most important questions about ____ **are simple ones.**

_____ **, and if so,** _____?

how
what
where
why
when

Only by answering these questions _____ _____.[1]

(invert subject/verb order)

Notes

1. _In the last sentence, you must put the verb before the subject (_can we, will you, _etc.) because the sentence starts with_ Only by. _This is advanced grammar, and if you use it correctly, you will impress your reader._

Question: Recently, there has been a lot of worry about avian flu. Do you think this is a serious problem for the world?

Example

The most important questions about avian flu **are simple ones**. Can we be made safe, **and if so,** how? **Only by answering these questions** _can we_ get a head start on planning for the disaster that everyone is predicting.

Question: Do you think that the famous Thai resort of Phuket can recover from the devastation of the 2005 tsunami?

Example

> **The most important questions about** the renovation of Phuket after the tsunami **are simple ones**. Can the resort and its beaches be made safe, **and if so,** how? **Only by answering these questions** *can progress be made* toward revitalizing the tourist trade.

Your Question: What are some important qualities of a good school teacher? Use specific details and examples to explain why these qualities are important.

Your Example

_____

_____

_____

Your Question: Some music is very inspirational. Other music seems boring and meaningless. Which type of music do you listen to, and why do you think some music forms are much more popular than others?

Your Example

_____

_____

_____

➔ ## II. INTRODUCTION WITH QUESTIONS TEMPLATES

What Is Introduction Templates

Introduction templates 4–6 do not need a roadmap template because the questions you ask set up the organization for the essay. We will begin with an introduction template that is just an extension of the thesis sentence templates you have done. This template is to be used when the topic is not a proposition but rather a question beginning with *What is X?*

> **What _____ X _____ is is a/an _____ question.**
>
> > fascinating
> > difficult
> > tough
> > thought-provoking
> > interesting
> > multi-dimensional
> > provocative
>
> **It raises further questions[1]: When _____?**
>
> **Where _____? How _____? Why _____?**
>
> **What _____?**

Question: What is culture?[2]

Example

> **What** culture **is is**[3] a provocative **question. It raises further questions:**
> **Where** do we find culture? **How** do we distinguish high culture from
> low culture? **What** is the difference between culture and ordinary
> behavior?

Question: What is comedy?

Example

> **What** comedy **is is** a fascinating **question. It raises further questions:**
> **Why** do we put plays into the categories of tragedy, comedy, and
> tragicomedy? **When** did people start writing comedies? **Where** was
> comedy first performed?

Notes

1. *You must decide what further questions will be raised. You don't need to ask three questions. You might just ask two. Or you could ask four. The template has the additional benefit of organizing the body of your paper, since you now have a paragraph to write for each question.*

2. *Use this template only with short* What is *questions like,* What is culture? *If you attempt to use it with longer questions like,* What is the biggest risk you have taken in the last five years? *the syntax becomes unwieldy and awkward.*

3. *Your computer's grammar checker may indicate that this construction is faulty because* is *is followed by another* is. *Your computer would be in error. The first* is *is part of a noun clause that forms the subject:* What X is. *This noun clause takes the verb* is. *Using this structure establishes your mastery of some sophisticated English syntax. This template is recommended for stronger writers.*

4. *Remember to begin with* What X is is. . . . *Do not use question form in this noun clause. In other words, do not say, for example,* What is comedy is. . . .

Your Question: What is air pollution?

Your Example

_____

_____

_____

Your Question: What is true love?

Your Example

_____

_____

_____

Why, Who, and *What Do/Does* Template

This template is largely the same as the previous one, but the structure is changed slightly in order to answer a *why* question, a *who* question, or a *what does/do* question.

_____ _____ **is a/an** _____ **question.**

Why   fascinating
What   difficult
Who   tough
                                       thought-provoking
                                       interesting
                                       multi-dimensional
                                       provocative

It raises further questions: When _____?[1]

Where _____? **How** _____? **What**_____?[2]

Question: Why are some people blue-eyed while others are brown-eyed?

Example

Why some people are blue-eyed while others are brown-eyed **is a** thought-provoking **question. It raises further questions: Why** do people have different hair and skin colors? **What** is a recessive gene? **Which** parent passes on eye-color genes?

Question: Why are French films so popular in America?

Example

Why French films are so popular in America **is a** fascinating **question. It raises further questions: Which** French directors are most popular? **How** do distributors of movies decide which French films to distribute in America? **When** did French cinema become popular in America?

Question: Who was the most influential person in your life?

Example

Who the most influential person in my life **was is[3] a** tough **question. It raises further questions: Why** should there be one most influential person, rather than two or several? **When** did this person enter my life and exert his/her influence? **Why** does this person stand out above all the other influential people in my life?

Question: What do you want to be doing 20 years from now?

Example

What I want to be doing 20 years from now **is an** interesting **question. It raises further questions: What** is my ultimate goal in life? **Where** do I want to live? **When** should I start a family?

Your Question: Why is it important to eat a balanced diet?

Your Example

_____

_____

_____

Your Question: Why do people seem to act more crazy when the moon is full?

Your Example

_____

_____

_____

Your Question: Who is the most successful businessperson in your country?

Your Example

_____

_____

_____

Your Question: What do people do for fun in your hometown?

Your Example

_____

_____

_____

Notes

1. *As with all templates, you can change the tense. For example, When was . . . ? Who has been . . . ?*
2. *You can use any questions in the last line of the template and in any order. You could use two, three, or four questions, as you will notice in the examples.*
3. *Notice that there are two forms of the verb* to be *back to back (e.g., is is or was is). This is the correct way to structure the noun clause answer. Doing this correctly may be difficult, but it shows that you can handle a difficult structure.*

Do You Think Introduction Template

This template is not for the beginning writer or the timid writer because it demands some syntactic manipulation. If you understand how it works, then by all means use it. Many essay questions ask: *Do you think that . . . ?* or *Do you agree that . . . ?* When you write your template, ignore these words and use the words that appear in the *that* clause. So, if the question were: *Do you think that hot dogs are good?* you would write: *Whether hot dogs are good or not. . . .*

Whether _____ _____ **or not is a/an** _____ **question.**

fascinating
difficult
tough
thought-provoking
interesting
multi-dimensional
provocative

It raises further questions: When _____**?**

Where _____**? How** _____**? Why** _____**?**

What _____**?**[1]

Question: Do you think that aliens exist?

Example

> **Whether** aliens exist **or not is a** fascinating **question. It raises further questions**: **How** would they react to us? **Where** did they come from? **Why** did they come to our planet?

Question: Should we have more nuclear power plants instead of relying on oil?

Example

Whether we have more nuclear power plants **or not is a** provocative **question. It raises further questions**: **What** are the dangers of nuclear power plants? **How** much oil is left in the ground? **Is** solar power an alternative to nuclear power?

Note

1. *Questions of all kinds can be added to the template. In the last example you will notice a question beginning with* Is.

Your Question: Do you think that all students should go to college?

Your Example

_____

_____

_____

Your Question: Do you think boxing should be banned?

Your Example

_____

_____

_____

➔ III. ROADMAP TEMPLATES

If your introduction does not already spell out how your essay will be organized, then you need a roadmap. Roadmaps are used in writing for almost all academic journals. It is surprising, then, that roadmaps are seldom taught in high school or college writing courses. Your writing will sound more professional when you use a roadmap. You will also see that a roadmap is a fail-safe measure that ensures proper organization. You create your roadmap as you develop your essay, and you may change it often as you revise your content and the order in which you develop your ideas.

Roadmap Template for Question Introduction

Begin your essay with this template. It starts with a question, and that can be your introduction. Or you may begin with some general words about the Question, then use the roadmap in the same paragraph.

_____ _____?

Do/Does

Is/Are

Has/Have

The goal of this _____ is _____.

       study
       paper
       analysis
       essay

To this end, this _____ is organized in _____ sections.

paper	one
study	two
review	three
essay	four
	five

The first section _____ _____.

> examines
> describes
> identifies
> explores
> shows
> details
> deals with
> compares

The second section _____.

(same list as under first section_)_

The final section _____.

(same list as under first section_)_

Question: How have you grown and developed over the four years of your high school career?

Example

Have I grown and developed over the four years of my high school career? **The goal of this** essay **is** to document why my answer to this question is a definitive yes. **To this end, this** essay **is organized in** three **sections. The first section** examines my growth and development as a budding scholar. **The second section** explores my development as an athlete. **The final section** details how I have developed emotionally, as an empathic human being.

Question: Write about your favorite book or film and tell how it has influenced you.

Example

Is there one favorite book or film that stands out as a strong influence on me? **The goal of this** essay **is** to illustrate how the novel _All The Stars Came Out That Night_ has been so influential in my personal development. **To this end, this** essay **is organized in** three **sections. The first section** deals with the issue of race in that novel and in my life. **The second section** examines the theme of courage in the novel and in my life. **The final section** shows how class was an issue in the novel and how it influenced my dealing with being from a low class.

Roadmap Template Examples with Student Errors

Some examples of introduction/roadmap template 1 follow. The thesis is expressed in the first sentence as a question. No corrections have been made. You can see how students actually used the template. The first is by a native speaker. The others are by international graduate students during their first year in the United States. The thesis sentences generally speak to the work the students are engaged in. In some cases, I provided a short list of possibilities for students who couldn't think of something to write about. This writing was done simply as part of an exercise in creating introductions. Students did not write an entire paper on these topics. These international students had never taken a writing course in the United States. In some cases, there are significant errors. But as a whole, all of the introductions work—you can understand what the papers by non-native speakers are about, and without the template you probably would not have been able to understand what they were about. The native speaker was a very good writer, an undergraduate engineering student. He wrote a comical piece, but notice how well the humor is set up by the organizing principles inherent in the template.

(native speaker)

1. **Do** fish swim or are they actually motorcyclists? **The goal of this paper is** to demonstrate how fish have evolved to use motorcycles. **To this end, the paper is organized in three main sections: The first section describes** the fish tail, clearly intended to be used for motorcycle turn signals. **The second section explores** the use of scale colors as part of a complicated right-of-way system. **The final section examines** lessons we can learn from the perfect harmony of a motorcycle-based aquatic society.

    (continued)

(non-native speakers)

2. **Does** the sensation of pain benefit an organism or is it a bad feeling? **The goal of this essay is organized in three sections: The first section shows** how people can benefit from the painful sensation. **The second section describes** the up to date data about how bad the sensation pain is. **The final section tries** to provide my personal view on the topic, which is that acute pain is an alarming signal to warn the organisms the potential danger, while organisms can rarely benefit from the chronic pain, which can last months or even years, sometimes leading people to suicide.

3. **Are** people optimists or pessimists? **The goal of this study is to describe** if the majority of people are positive in their moods. **To this end, this study is organized in three sections. The first section describes** a simple experiment alone on a significant statistical population. The experiment tried to make people miss the train. **The second section analyzes** the behavior of the people that swear in stead of remain calm. **The final section reported** a statistical correlation finding that the majority of the considered population got angry.

4. **Do** university students spend more time working or socializing? **The goal of this study is to reveal** student perceptions of time spent studying and socializing. **To this end, this paper is organized into two sections. The first section examines** the ratio of true time spent studying to time spend socializing. **The second section compares** this ratio to student perceptions. **Finally, . . .**

5. **Do** men and women think and talk differently, and is it difficult to understand each other? **The goal of this paper is** to know what is the difference of men and women and about the method to understand people who has opposite sex. **To this end, this paper is organized in three sections. The first section shows** that men usually talk with their male friends to gather informations and to find of solutions of some problems. **The second section describes** that women usually talk with their female friend to remove the stress and to get the agreement of some problems. **The final section identifies** that men should be listen to women's talking.

6. **Is** driving by myself to work useful? **The goal of this analysis is to illustrate** its serious usefulness. **To this end, the reasons are organized in three sentences/sections. First one.** it is a very long distance between my apartment and Brandeis. **Second one.** the public transportation is very poor in the USA. **Third one.** the public bus/rail is often delayed, even be cancelled. **So** driving with my car to Brandeis is very/really useful and important.

7. **Does** the dam help a country, or does it make a country into a more dangerous situation? **The goal of this paper is to discuss** this question. **To this end, the paper is organized in three sections: The first section** the amount of electric power the dam will give to the country. **The second section estimates** the results of flood caused by land sliding. **The final section shows** the feeling of all types of people in that country to the dam.

Your Question: Write about a person who has had an influence on you, and describe that influence.

Your Example

_____

_____

_____

_____

Your Question: The 20th century had many of famous people who helped change our world. Who do you think made the greatest change in the world? Why?

Your Example

Question Series Introduction/Roadmap

If you are taking a standardized test, begin with the question you are being asked. Then, add a few additional questions that the topic raises and that you are going to discuss. This provides the organization of your essay. This template is more suited to argumentative essays, but the first template example shows how it can be used in personal narrative essays. You can, of course, omit any part of the template that does not fit your topic. Notice that the first template example omits the sentence: *My _____ is that _____.*

Is _____?

Does _____?

When/where/why does _____?

This _____ _____ **to answer these** _____ **questions.**

paper	tries	difficult
essay	attempts	intriguing
narrative		tough
		fascinating
		beguiling

My _____ **is that** _____.

argument
opinion
thesis
narrative

I will _____ **my** _____ **with examples** _____ _____.

support	argument	from
develop	opinion	of
	thesis	
	narrative	

Note

As an alternative to the fourth sentence (This paper . . .), you could use this different structure:

Answers to these questions will be _____ in the following paragraphs.

> undertaken
> offered
> suggested

Question: Review your reasons for attending college. Explain how earning a college degree will help fulfill your career goals.

Example

What are the reasons for attending Harrad College? **How** will earning a college degree help fulfill my career goals? **What**, indeed, are my career goals? **Answers to these questions will be** undertaken **in the following paragraphs. I will** develop **my** narrative **with examples** of how I achieved previous goals and how these goals are linked to my future.

Question: Futurist Ray Kurzweil sees technology immensely changing the way we live in just a few decades. How do you think technology will change the way we live in the next thirty years?

Example

How will technology change the way we live in the next 30 years? **Will** our lives be better? **Will** we coexist with millions of robots? **Will** I fall in love with a cyborg? **Will** we create weapons of mass destruction and annihilate life on earth? **This** essay attempts **to answer these** intriguing **questions. My** opinion **is that** technological change is inevitable, but we face many dangers. **I will** support **my** opinion **with examples** of how I think life will be in the year 2035.

Your Question: Some futurists take a dim view of life in a world where our brain power is amplified a million times by computer chips inserted into our brains. They say, for one, that we should not allow this to happen unless we find ways to deal with the ethical problems in such a world, ways to keep religion in our lives. What is your opinion?

Your Example

_____

_____

_____

_____

Your Question: One of the problems faced by Europe is a decrease in population. In some countries, for every two people who die, only one is being born. Do you think this is a big problem? Why or why not? If it is, what can be done about it?

Your Example

_____

_____

_____

_____

Argument Roadmap Template 1[1]

This _____ _____ _____.

     essay   challenges

     paper   examines

                    argues

                    maintains.

It _____ **first** _____.

   questions

   examines

   maintains

   argues

Then it points out _____.

It contends, further, that _____.

It concludes that _____.[2]

Question: Some high schools require all students to wear the same uniforms. Other high schools allow students to wear whatever they want. Which way do you think is better? Uniforms or anything the students want?

Example

This essay challenges the idea that all students should be required to wear the same uniforms. **It** questions **first** why administrators want to make everybody look the same. **Then it points out** that diversity is a goal, not only in the make-up of the student body but in the clothes students wear. **It contends, further, that** choosing the clothes you wear is an expression of free speech, defended by the Constitution. **It concludes that** sameness[3] in anything is a bad idea.

Question: Some people say that the 20th century saw more change in the world than any other century before it. Do you agree or disagree?

Example

This paper argues that the 20th century saw more change in the world than any other century before it. **It** questions **first** which centuries might come close as times of change. **Then it points out** that change is exponential. **It contends, further, that** change comes largely from science, and there are many more scientists now than in any other century. **It concludes that** the 21st century will probably see even more change than the 20th.

Your Question: A company has just announced that it plans on opening a very large shopping center in your neighborhood. Do you think this is a good plan or bad plan?

Your Example

_____

_____

_____

_____

Your Question: In some parts of the world there are still arranged marriages—marriages made by parents or relatives for men and women who might not even know each other. Do you think these marriages can work as well as, or better than, marriages made directly between the man and the woman?

Your Example

_____

_____

_____

_____

Notes

1. *This template should be used when your essay is an argument (for or against something). It cannot be used, unless you modify it, when you are writing about personal experience—for instance, about* The book that most influenced you.
2. *Notice that the template has five parts, each one a paragraph. There is an introduction, three body paragraphs, and a conclusion.*
3. *You need to think about your conclusion before you finish this template. You can come back to the line,* It concludes . . . *after you write your conclusion, if you so desire.*

Argument Roadmap Template 2

The previous argument template (pages 55–56) was taken from the abstract of an article I wrote for a psychological journal. Shortly after extrapolating that template, I read the introduction of a chapter written by a prominent philosopher. This argument roadmap template, derived from that introduction, is remarkably similar. The lesson here is that native speakers have much of the same syntax in their heads and it produces very similar introductions, so there is no reason that you should not use the same syntax.

This _____ _____ _____.

     essay   examines

     chapter   details

     paper

Beginning with _____,

it goes on to _____.

It proceeds to _____.

All told, the _____ **illustrates** _____.[1]

      essay

      chapter

      paper

Question: Agree or disagree with the following statement. It is better for a woman to help her husband with his career than to have a career herself.

Example

This essay examines whether it is better for a woman to help her husband with his career than to have a career herself. **Beginning with** a disagreement with the statement on the basis of equal rights, **it goes on to** argue that if there is a divorce after many years, the woman would have no way to support herself if she just helped her husband with his career. **It proceeds to** say that money is power, and if you don't earn money, you have little power in a marriage. **All told, the** essay **illustrates** the need for equality in all human relationships.

Question: You have just finished writing your 300-page autobiography. Please submit page 217.

Example

> **This** page of my autobiography details a traumatic incident in my life. **Beginning with** my first date, at age 15, **it goes on to** describe my date's father, who had a hand like a catcher's mitt. **It proceeds to** tell why he threatened to kill me if I ever darkened his door again. **All told, the** page **illustrates** why you should never date girls whose fathers are butchers.

Your Question: Relate the most humorous experience in your life.

Your Example

_____

_____

_____

_____

Your Question: Do you think English is the most important language in the world?

Your Example

_____

_____

_____

_____

Note

1. *Again, the five paragraph structure is indicated.* All told *begins your conclusion.* All told *is a short way of saying,* When everything is told. *Using this expression distinguishes you as a competent writer.*

Roadmap Template without First Person

Because some high school teachers do not allow students to use the first person (though they seldom specify singular or plural—*I* or *we*), we offer this template. Along with some of the preceding templates, this one allows you to write without using the first person. This template can be used when you have only two topics to discuss in the body of your paper, but it could also be used with a much longer essay.

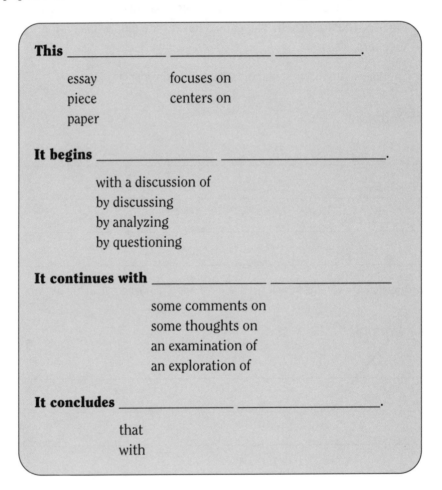

This _____ _____ _____.

    essay   focuses on
    piece   centers on
    paper

It begins _____ _____.

    with a discussion of
    by discussing
    by analyzing
    by questioning

It continues with _____ _____

    some comments on
    some thoughts on
    an examination of
    an exploration of

It concludes _____ _____.

    that
    with

Question: Discuss some issue of personal, local or national concern and why it is important to you.

Example

This essay focuses on a matter of national concern—the reconstruction of New Orleans after Hurricane Katrina, which is important to me personally. **It begins** by analyzing what went wrong in the aftermath of the hurricane. **It continues with** some thoughts on what remains to be done. **It concludes** that we are not ready for next year's hurricane season.

Question: If you had the chance to meet a famous person, past or present, who would it be, and why?

Example

This essay centers on a very famous person whom I would love to meet but can't because she is dead: Marilyn Monroe. **It begins** with a discussion of the actress's marvelous personality. **It continues with** an exploration of her appeal to millions of red-blooded Americans. **It concludes** that such a meeting should be in a cozy bistro with a bottle of Dom Perignon champagne.

Your Question: If you had the chance to meet a famous person, past or present, who would it be, and why?"

Your Example

_____

_____

_____

_____

Your Question: Do you think all university students should be required to study art and learn a musical instrument? Why or why not?

Your Example

_____

_____

_____

_____

Contrasting Views Roadmap Template

With this template, you dispose of one or more competing views in order to advance your own view. The idiom *giving the devil his due* is a colorful one, meaning "paying attention to what the other side is saying." The fourth line *(while . . .)* counters the opposing argument. This template is more difficult than some of the preceding ones because it demands that you look at both sides of an issue. If you can't do it, just skip this one. However, if you are capable of looking at both sides, this template will help you to organize your answer, and it will impress the reader. *Take heed of* means "pay attention to."

> **In this essay, I will** _____.
>
> **Giving the devil his due, I will** _____ **that**
>
> take on the argument(s)
take heed of the opposing
arguments
>
> _____.
>
> **I will conclude that, while** _____ **X** _____, _____ **Y** _____.[1]

Note

1. *X and Y must be contrasting ideas; X is the devil's due, while Y is your point of view.*

Question: Should all students be allowed to go to college if they so wish?

Example

In this essay, I will argue that not all students who want to go to college should actually go. **Giving the devil his due, I will** take on the argument **that** students who do poorly in high school came from disadvantaged backgrounds and had bad teachers. **I will conclude that, while** our educational system deprives some worthy students of the opportunity to go to college, our system is a lot fairer than that of most countries.

Question: Should all students be allowed to go to college if they so wish?

Example

> **In this essay, I will** argue that all students who wish to go to college should be allowed to go. **Giving the devil his due, I will** take heed of the opposing argument **that** some students are naturally disruptive or just plain stupid[1]. **I will conclude that, while** it may take disadvantaged students longer to finish college, they can do it if given a chance.

Your Question: Agree or disagree with the following statement. Children should be required to do household tasks as soon as they are able to.

Your Example

_____

_____

_____

_____

Your Question: If you were an employer, which kind of employee would you prefer to hire: an inexperienced worker at a lower salary or an experienced worker at a higher salary?

Your Example

_____

_____

_____

_____

Note

 1. *This template can be expanded by adding one line* (while . . .). *The same template with the new line added, as shown on page 64.*

In this essay, I will _____.

Giving the devil his due, I will _____ **that**

> take on the argument(s)
> take heed of the opposing
> arguments

_____,

while _____ **that** _____.

> noting
> pointing out

I will conclude that, while ____X____ , ____Y____ .

Example

In this essay, I will argue that not all students who want to go to college should actually go. **Giving the devil his due, I will** take on the arguments **that** students who do poorly in high school came from disadvantaged backgrounds and had poor teachers, **while** noting **that** many of these students are sociopaths and hooligans. **I will conclude that, while** our educational system deprives some worthy students of the opportunity to go to college, our system is a lot fairer than that of most countries.

Advanced Roadmap Template

If you are a good writer and you are writing a longer paper, consider using this more elaborate roadmap template. You should feel free to omit any lines you want, except the first.

My purpose in this _____ **is** _____,

       paper
       analysis
       essay

focusing especially on _____,

pointing out that _____,

and concentrating on _____.

Along the way, I will _____ _____.

       delve into
       note that
       take into consideration
       look at
       examine
       pay attention to

I will further support my thesis that _____
with _____.

Evidence for my _____ **will come from** _____.

       argument
       point of view

Example

My purpose in this paper **is** to determine whether couples therapy works, **focusing especially on** the outcomes of the therapy, **pointing out that** many couples drop out of therapy, **and concentrating on** withdrawal of the man or the woman. **Along the way, I will** delve into the coding of couples' conversations. **I will further support my thesis**

that success of couples' therapy depends mostly on the couple's active participation in the process **with** data from my research.. **Evidence for my** argument **will come from** transcripts of voice recordings of couples in therapy.

Roadmap for Long Paper

This is a template for a long paper, a research paper. It is taken directly from the paper of an international graduate student, and the example is from her paper.

> **I will begin by** _____.
>
> **This will lead to** _____.
>
> **Next,** _____.
>
> **I will then** _____.
>
> **Next, I will turn my attention to** _____.
>
> **I will conclude** _____.

Example

I will begin by discussing different theories and development policies that attempt to deal with poverty. **This will lead to** a discussion of small-scale enterprises and cooperatives, both formal and informal. **Next,** I will evaluate the impact of cooperatives and show that women can participate in business as effectively as men can. **I will then** indicate strategies which could support women's efforts. Such strategies, however, may be ineffective without adequate credit, and I will discuss the role of banks in helping small-scale women's enterprises. **Next, I will turn my attention to** the particular case of South Africa in the wake of the recent global conference in which black and white women participated for the first time. **I will conclude** that prospects for real change and for implementation of the strategies that could help small-scale enterprise in South Africa are cloudy.

Conclusion Templates

No better advice on conclusions can be given than William Germano's remark: "If the first rule of writing is 'Begin strong,' the other first rule is 'Close well.' Every novelist knows that the end is where you pull the pieces together or the whole craft sinks."[1] Alas, conclusions are often poorly taught in high school, where they tend to consist of restatement, self-congratulation, and wildly unsubstantiated global claims. In college, most students learn to extend their conclusions to a wider context. Students are also encouraged to ask a provocative question, which by itself expands the thesis to a wider context. Some texts advise students to suggest a solution, make a prediction, or make a recommendation. In most cases, the solution should have been dealt with in the body of the paper, not in the conclusion.

So, to review, the conclusion can briefly restate the thesis, extend the thesis to other contexts, and ask a provocative question (or questions). Pay attention also to Carla Zecher's advice: "A conclusion is often the best place to address the 'so what?' factor: why has it been important for someone to write this . . . , and why is it important for someone to read it?"[2]

These strategies, however valuable, ignore a very important facet of conclusions in most professional writing: that is, discussing the limitations of what you have done and pointing the way for future writing on that subject. The focus on limitations may apply to personal narrative as well as to argumentative writing.

A writer of an argumentative piece puts herself or himself in a scholarly continuum. This means dealing with what came before you and what will come after you. As for the former, this means citing the sources used in the research. You realize, of course, that yours is not the last word on any subject. Others will write about that subject in the future, and with personal narrative, *you* may write more on the subject. Therefore, your conclusion should take on an air of humility, not of self-congratulation. There is always more to be done, and your writing represents only the slightest addition to the world's sum of knowledge on any topic. So, what should you do? You should reflect on what you have <u>not</u> done and lead future writers to paths that you have not taken but

---

[1]William Germano, "Final Thoughts," *Profession*, no. 1 (2005): 176.
[2]Carla Zecher, "Openings and Endings of Scholarly Books," *Profession*, no. 1 (2005): 168.

could prove fruitful. In a word, let us say that the focus of your conclusion should be: *limitations*.

Now, since few high school students and only a small fraction of college students do this, you will be well ahead of the game if you do it. And it should make you proud and/or happy to put yourself into this wider context of contributing something, however small, to the sum of thinking about a certain topic. You will be thinking and writing at a higher level as a result.

Of course, since you may never have done this before, these general words will mean little in the practical realm unless you are a budding genius. To help you along with the process of learning how to write a professional-sounding conclusion, you now have templates.

Very Short Conclusion Templates

If you have difficulty memorizing the longer templates, here are some two-line templates that are easy to remember. These templates are recommended for use in the Integrated Writing Task of the TOEFL® iBT, where you respond to a reading with summary and paraphrase rather than construct your own essay.

1a. Two-Line Conclusion Template

> **To recapitulate, what we have here is an exposition of _____.**
>
> **The intriguing ideas expressed here open the door to questions about _____.**

1b. Two-Line Conclusion Template

> **To recapitulate, what we have here is an exposition of _____.**
>
> **Of further interest in this regard is _____.**

1c. Two-Line Conclusion Template

> **To recap, what we have here is an exposition of _____.**
>
> **This intriguing subject stimulates questions such as _____.**

Example Thesis: Cats have given rise to many interesting expressions in English.

Examples

1a. **To recapitulate, what we have here is an exposition of** how cats have entered the English language. **The intriguing ideas expressed here open the door to questions about** how other animals have influenced the English language.

1b. **To recapitulate, what we have here is an exposition of** how cats have entered the English language. **Of further interest in this regard is** how other animals have influenced the English language.

1c. **To recap, what we have here is an exposition of** how cats have entered the English language. **This intriguing subject stimulates questions such as** how other animals have influenced the English language.

Your Thesis: Hormones produced by new techniques are very useful in treating many blood-related diseases.

Your Conclusions

a. _____

_____

_____

_____

b. _____

_____

_____

_____

c. _____

_____

_____

_____

Rhetorical Question Conclusion Template 1

This template points out the limitations of what you have done with a question. The question is called "rhetorical" because it is not a true question. It is an answer in the guise of a question. Note that the subject and verb can be made plural *(Is this/Are these)*. After the first template, you need to expand the new thought—explain it and perhaps give examples.

Is this the only possible _____ _____?

interpretation of
choice in/of
solution for/of
course of action in

Of course not. _____.

Example

Are these the only possible interpretations of the play? **Of course not**. Understanding Beckett's mastery of symbolism and stagecraft is only the beginning. We could go down the road of puns, playing with language. That's the road Godot took, isn't it? *Did-I go-go*? There is also the road that connects Beckett to his forebears, that connects Ireland to England. Beckett's landscape may appear bare, but beneath the surface, there is much to be mined.

Your Turn: Try writing a short conclusion with this template. The thesis of your essay is given.

Your Thesis: Though you have eaten little international food, you have chosen Chinese dumplings as the best Asian dish.

Your Example

Is this the only possible _____? Of course not.

_____

_____.

Rhetorical Question Conclusion Template 2

> But is this the whole story? What _____ **X** ?[1]
>
> $\qquad\qquad\qquad\qquad$ if
> $\qquad\qquad\qquad\qquad$ about
>
> As this and other such questions suggest, _____ **Y** _____.[2] [3]

Notes

1. *X represents something you have left out, something else about the topic that someone else could talk about. In Y, you should develop the idea of X to a slight degree.*
2. *This does not have to be the entirety of your conclusion. You could begin with a short restatement of the thesis and then use this template.*
3. *This template works best with argumentative essays.*

Example

The thesis has been that smoking should be banned in public places.

> **But is this the whole story? What** about smoking in places that are not public or that are quasi-public? **As this and other such questions suggest**, protecting the public from the dangers of smoking is a battle with many fronts.

Example

The thesis has been that high school students should be required to wear uniforms.

> **But is this the whole story?**[1] **What** about elementary school children? **As this and other such questions suggest**, the same reasons that make uniforms a good idea in high school should apply to other educational divisions.

Note

1. *Your question here is rhetorical; that is, you do not think that the preceding is the whole story. You must think of something besides what has been said, and that is your X. It doesn't matter much what your subject is. I challenge my students to find a subject that cannot be concluded with templates like this one. One student challenged me to write a conclusion about gummy bears (a kind of candy). Here goes:*

   > **But is this the whole story? What** about the fattening effects of gummy bears? **As this and other such questions suggest**, gummy bears are particularly insidious when it comes to making kids fat.

Your Thesis: Students should be allowed to go to all museums free at all times.

Your Conclusion

_____

_____

_____

_____

Your Thesis: You have argued that it is better to spend money on buying a house than on buying a business.

Your Conclusion

_____

_____

_____

_____

Rhetorical Question Conclusion Template 2a

This is a variation of the preceding template, with the second line changed.

But is this the whole story? What _____ ___**X**___ **?**

if
about

Now we find ourselves with a richer story, one that
_____ _____ .

shows
reveals
demonstrates

Example

The thesis has been that smoking should be banned in public places.

> **But is this the whole story? What** about smoking in places that are not public or that are quasi-public? **Now we find ourselves with a richer story, one that** reveals that smoking is a far greater risk than what tobacco companies would have you think and should be banned everywhere.

Example

The thesis has been that high school students should be required to wear uniforms.

> **But is this the whole story? What** about elementary school children? **Now we find ourselves with a richer story, one that** demonstrates that similarity of clothing for all grades levels the playing field so that students see only the differences in one another's ideas.

Example

> **But is this the whole story? What** about the fattening effects of gummy bears? **Now we find ourselves with a richer story, one that** reveals the possibility of becoming obese starting from a childhood full of gummy bears.

Your Thesis: The biggest risk you have ever taken is running for president of your senior class.

Your Conclusion

_____

_____

_____

_____

Your Thesis: You have argued that vending machines selling candy and other unhealthy food should not be allowed in high schools.

Your Conclusion

_____

_____

_____

_____

Conclusion Template 1

Here is a template with four different last sentences from which you may choose one. X represents the main points or facets you wrote about. Y is your topic. Z is what is left to discuss.

_____, let me recapitulate the main _____ of my _____.

To conclude   facets   narration
In conclusion   points   argument
                                                               comparison

_____**X**_____.

Obviously, not every issue related to __Y__ has been _____.

                                                               discussed
                                                               undertaken
                                                               examined.

What _____ for further _____ is/are ___Z___.

I leave   investigation
is left   commentary
remains   understanding
                   discussion

Note: _Here follow three variations of the last sentence. If you like one of these better, then substitute it for the last sentence._

Matters that have not been included here are _____Z_____.

These need to be investigated.

Or:

Matters that have not been investigated include ____Z____.

These matters also deserve _____.

                   our attention
                   the attention of other writers

on the _____.
          subject
          topic

> Or:
>
> What remains to be discussed at further length
> _____ _____Z_____.
>
> is the matter of
> are the matters of

Example Thesis: You have decided that the best way for you to do community service is to read to the blind.

Example

To conclude, **let me recapitulate the main** facets **of my** narration. Community service is vital for a thriving democracy, and all citizens should do it. Reading to the blind would be my choice of service. **Obviously, not every issue related to** community service **has been** discussed. **What** I leave **for further** commentary **is** an understanding of how the message of voluntary community service can be spread to the wealthy folks who would rather play golf.

Example Thesis: The things to do for good health are: get exercise avoid risky behavior and eat lots of green leafy vegetables.

Example

In conclusion, **let me recapitulate the main** points **of my** argument. To remain healthy, one should get exercise, avoid risky behaviors, and eat lots of green leafy vegetables like spinach. **Obviously, not every issue related to** good health **has been** examined. **What** remains **for further** discussion are the matters of vitamin supplements and the elimination of transfats from one's diet.

Your Thesis: One natural resource that is disappearing from Brazil is the rain forest.

Your Conclusion

_____

_____

_____

_____

Your Thesis: Advances in genetic science will bring a cure for cancer.

Your Conclusion

_____

_____

_____

_____

Argument Conclusion Template

In the first line you briefly restate your thesis. X represents some limitation of your argument. Y represents your topic.

What I have argued here is that _____.

However, I can't _____ **that** ___X___.

> say
> offer the comforting assurance

I have merely _____ _____Y_____.

> scratched the surface of
> noted that

_____ **about** _____Y_____.

Much more could written
More work remains to be done

For instance, _____.

Example Thesis: Rock music is more popular than classical music because people can dance to it.

Example

> **What I have argued here is that** rock music is more popular than classical music because it can be danced to. **However, I can't** offer the comforting assurance **that** this is the only reason for rock's greater popularity. **I have merely** scratched the surface of why rock is so popular. More work remains to be done **about** rock's popularity. **For instance,** musical genres are crossing now.

Example Thesis: Security is more important in life than freedom.

Conclusion

What I have argued here is that security is more important in my life than freedom because without the former the latter is impossible. **However, I can't** say **that** security is the most important thing in my life. **I have merely** noted that security plays a very important role. Much more could be written **about** the important things in life. **For instance**, some might say that all you need is love.

Your Thesis: Important qualities of a good teacher include patience and devotion to the craft of teaching.

Your Conclusion

_____

_____

_____

_____

Your Thesis: The Internet is the most important invention of all inventions.

Your Conclusion

_____

_____

_____

_____

Conclusion Template 2 (Effect)

This conclusion template can be used when something has had an effect on something else. X is your topic here. Y is an example of the effect that X has had.

Clearly, __X__ has/have had a _____ effect on _____.

> strong
> significant
> great

In short, if ____Y____ is/are any indication, ____X____ will continue to _____. Only further _____ will _____.

> studies   determine
> investigation   show
> research

Example Thesis: The movie that had the biggest influence on me was *The Chronicles of Narnia*.

Example

Clearly, *The Chronicles of Narnia* **has had** a strong **effect on** me. **In short, if** ticket sales **are any indication,** *The Chronicles of Narnia* **will continue to** have effects on thousands of kids. **Only further** investigation **will** show how this film will effect my appreciation of similar Biblical stories.

Example Thesis: An experience that had special meaning to me was discovering that Santa Claus was not real.

Example

Clearly, the discovery that Santa Claus was not real **has had a** significant **effect on** me. **In short, if** my experience with the myth of Santa Claus **is any indication,** kids **will continue to** uncover many truths that adults would rather they not discover. **Only further** studies **will** determine the effects, perhaps both positive and negative, of lying to children.

Your Thesis: Teachers should not be allowed to use any corporal punishment (beating).

Your Conclusion

_____

_____

_____

_____

Your Thesis: All students should have free tuition in college.

Your Conclusion

_____

_____

_____

_____

Strong Claim Conclusion Template

This template is useful when you have made a strong claim.

_____ **be** _____.

My claim(s) will not	easy to accept
I have no illusions that my claim(s) will	palatable to all
	acceptable to all

_____ **the** _____ **part will be** _____.

Perhaps	hardest
Probably	most difficult
Indeed,	most challenging

Above all, I hope that _____ **can help to** _____.

this paper
this analysis
this criticism
this exploration

Thesis Example: More money should be spent on the poor and less on space research.

Example

My claims will not **be** palatable to all. Perhaps **the** hardest **part will be** my preference for giving poor students scholarships to college rather than sending a man to Mars. **Above all, I hope that** this exploration **can help to** reinvigorate the advocates of poor people.

Thesis Example: More money should not be spent on the poor at the expense of space research.

Example

I have no illusion that my claim will **be** acceptable to all, especially to card-carrying liberals. Probably **the** most challenging **part will be** convincing the less adventurous that we may find life on Mars. **Above all, I hope that** this analysis **can help to** refocus our attention on space, the last frontier, to get us to go where no man has gone before.

Your Thesis: Opening a big shopping center in my neighborhood is (not) a good plan.

Your Conclusion

_____

_____

_____

_____

Your Thesis: Students in all non–English speaking countries should (not) be required to study English.

Your Conclusion

_____

_____

_____

_____

Conclusion Template 3

In the first sentence (after *that*), you restate your thesis. *Longitudinal study* refers to study that takes several years to finish.

I do not suppose that _____.

I do expect that _____,

and I hope that _____.

Only _____ will prove, or disprove, what I think

    longitudinal study
    time
    further investigation
    further study

is the case—that _____.

Thesis Example: Writing templates are a good way to teach writing.

Example

I do not suppose that all writing teachers will immediately embrace the template approach. **I do expect that** time will turn the tide, as both native and non-native students, as well as tutors for SAT® and TOEFL® writing, embrace the approach, **and I hope that** writing teachers will use templates as a way of letting students discover on their own the syntactical structures of good essays. **Only** longitudinal study **will prove, or disprove, what I think is the case—that** students who use templates for various parts of their papers will eventually lose their need for templates and that the various syntactic structures that compose many good conclusions, introductions, etc., will be imprinted in the heads of the students who used templates to a much greater degree than in the heads of the students who never used them.

Thesis Example: The washing machine was the greatest invention of the 20th century.

Example

> **I do not suppose that** people who have never washed clothes by hand will agree with me. **I do expect that** the elderly will wholeheartedly accept my thesis, **and I hope that** younger folk will listen to the stories of their grandmothers or great-grandmothers, who worked their fingers to the bone and spent countless hours washing clothes by hand. **Only** further study **will prove, or disprove, what I think is the case—that** millions of hours have been saved by women who have washing machines.

Your Thesis: Big drug companies should sell their products to very poor countries at a fraction of the price they charge in the United States.

Your Conclusion

_____

_____

_____

_____

Your Thesis: Lotteries are bad because they encourage very poor people to spend their money on tickets when they have almost no chance of winning.

Your Conclusion

_____

_____

_____

_____

Advanced Conclusion Template

X represents an exaggeration of your claim, what is not included in it. Y represents your claim. This template demands the perhaps tricky feat of creating an exaggeration of your claim in order to show the limitation of that claim. If the examples do not sufficiently show you the way, do not use this one.

I do not claim that _____ **X** _____ .	
On the contrary, _____ **Y** _____ .	
Nonetheless, _____ .	
Only further _____ **will** _____ .	

studies	determine
examination	show
research	

Example Thesis: Einstein is the 20th century person who made the greatest change in the world.

Example

> **I do not claim that** Einstein was the only great agent of change in the 20th century. **On the contrary**, he was part of a brilliant cadre of physicists. **Nonetheless**, I would not hesitate to put him at the top of the list of people responsible for change. **Only further** studies in physics **will** determine Einstein's impact on the 21st century.

Example Thesis: I do not think that all students should go to college.

Example

> **I do not claim that** only the elite, the best and the brightest, should go to college. **On the contrary**, many more students than actually do go to college now have the intelligence to do so. **Nonetheless**, there are many students who dislike studying or who don't believe that college is worth the investment, and they should not go to college. **Only further** research **will** show whether vocational schools or military service are good alternatives to college.

Your Thesis: All students should be given the choice of going to college or not.

Your Conclusion

_____

_____

_____

_____

BODY OF PAPER TEMPLATES

Templates are easily suited to thesis sentences, introductions, and conclusions because the function of each of these is clear and distinct. The form that the body of your paper takes, on the other hand, is quite dependent on the content of that paper, so templates are not easily found. These difficulties notwithstanding, here are two short body templates that can be used in an essay that argues, discusses, or explains.

Body Template, Last Paragraph

The standard essay has five paragraphs, of which Paragraphs 2, 3, and 4 comprise the body. A good way to begin your last body paragraph is with one of the following (a, b, or c):

a. Any _____ **of** _____ _____ **would be**

      explanation   the fact that

      discussion

incomplete without mention of _____**.**

b. Not to mention _____ **would be** _____**.**

                                    an error

                                    a mistake

                                    an oversight

c. To omit from our discussion _____

                                that

                                the fact that

_____ **would be** _____**.**

      an error

      a mistake

      an oversight

Examples

Here is the last body paragraph of a sample essay response that was rated a 4 (from *The Michigan Guide to English for Academic Success and Better TOEFL® Test Scores,* page 176). See how the diction level with the template raises <u>this sentence</u> to level 5 (the student's introductory phrase, a transition *According to the lecture* could be considered vapid).

According to the lecture, environmental sex determination has three kinds of sex types that are male, female, and both types.

> a. **Any** explanation **of** the fact that sex determination **would be incomplete without mention of** the three kinds of sex types: male, female, and both types.
> b. **Not to mention** that sex determination has three kinds of sex types that are male, female, and both types **would be** an oversight.
> c. **To omit from our discussion** that sex determination has three kinds of sex type—male, female, and both—**would be** an oversight.

Your Turn

Two other first sentences of last body paragraphs from the same source follow. Try to improve them with the use of the templates. The sentences may be imperfectly constructed, so you can make any changes you want. Note that not all sentences can be transformed with all three templates. For example, (a) does not work well with the following example, so you can only use (b) or (c).

Some other species, such as birds and butterflies, have totally different chromosomes.

b. _____

_____

c. _____

_____

Lately, people are thinking of cats as our friends.

a. (The topic that you are explaining is *the changing attitudes toward cats*.)

_____

_____

b. _____

_____

c. _____

_____

Body Template, Opposing Argument

In an essay with an argument, a good writer will present the opposing opinion and attempt to demolish it. It is often a good strategy to begin with this demolition and then present your case. Note that when you present the opposition's case, you should put forward the opposition's strongest point(s). You might begin the paragraph that takes on the opposing view with this template.

Proponents of the opposing view argue that _____.

In light of this, _____ **we conclude that** _____?

      shall

      must

Not necessarily. _____ **X** _____.[1]

Note

1. *In X, you attempt to demolish the opposition argument or at least put a good dent in it.*

Example Thesis: The minimum wage should not be raised from $5.15/hr. to $7/hr.

Example

Proponents of the opposite view argue that there hasn't been an increase in the minimum wage since 1997 and that inflation makes $5.15/hr. seem like nothing. **In light of this** must **we conclude that** raising the minimum wage is a good thing for our country? **Not necessarily**. First, most of the people making the minimum wage work in restaurants and they get good money from tips, and if we pay them more, then the price of a hamburger will go up and people will stop eating at restaurants, which is bad for the economy.

Example Thesis: Americans have a constitutional right to bear arms, which means that citizens can have any type of arm they think they need, including assault rifles like the AK-47 (Kalashnikov.)

Example

> **Proponents of the opposite view argue that** you don't need an assault rifle to hunt deer or to protect your home. **In light of this,** shall **we conclude that** these weapons should be banned? **Not necessarily.** First, if a guy breaks into your house with an assault rifle, you don't want to confront him with a pop-gun. You need an assault rifle, too. Second, you can't necessarily trust your neighbors, and by that I mean neighboring countries, too. What if hordes pour across our borders? How else will we deter them? And what about the terrorists coming down from Canada? I want to put more than a bee-bee in their butts.

Your Thesis: The minimum wage should be raised from $5.15/hr. to $7/hr.

Your Example

_____

_____

_____

_____

Your Thesis: Assault rifles should be banned in America.

Your Example

_____

_____

_____

_____

SUMMARY TEMPLATE

In high school and in college, students are often asked to write summaries. The TOEFL® Integrated Writing Task includes a 20-minute written response to a reading and a recorded lecture. This in effect calls for a summary. Let us see how a template can improve a mediocre piece of summary writing. One good way to structure a summary is to adapt a roadmap template. For instance:

The main point(s) here is that _____.

In addition, I wish to _____ **that** _____.

> point out
> note

Furthermore, of particular interest is the fact that _____.

Also _____ **is the fact that** _____.

> of importance
> noteworthy

The final _____ **that I would note is that** _____.

> fact
> point
> feature

This template calls for a thesis and four supporting points. You could eliminate the second and/or third one (*Furthermore . . .* or *Also . . .*), depending on how many supporting points you have.

This example comes from page 177 of *The Michigan Guide to English for Academic Success and Better TOEFL® Test Scores*, an excellent companion book to *The Writing Template Book*.

It is important to note that summaries do not need conclusions! So, I have deleted the last paragraph (*As I mentioned above, there are some types of sex determination, and we could say that they are amazing.*) Read the essay without the template, which is in bold print, then read it with the template. See what a difference the organizational feature of the template makes!

SAMPLE RESPONSE

The main point here is that there are some types of sex determination on the earth. It depends on the species.

In addition, I want to point out that the sex of human being is determined by the production of hormones. As everyone knows, every beings have DNA. In human case, the 23rd pair of chromosomes in the cell has influence to human sex. Human being has the X chromosome and the Y one. If the 23rd pair was XX, the human is female. On the other hand, if the pair was XY, the human is male. So the sex of human being is decided by the pair.

Also of importance is the fact that some kinds of fishes can change their own sex after they were born. The mechanism is unknown, but actually the sex can change from the male to female if there were only two males or females. Moreover, the tempareture of water influence to fish's sex. High tempareture bring them to male, low tempareture bring them to female, and middle tempareture bring them both sex.

The final feature that I would note is that some other species, such as birds and bataflies, have totally different chromosomes, W and Z. The mechanizm of sex determination is similar to human being, but of course it is not exactly some as humans because of types of chromosomes.